M000030896

Nobody *Loves You* Like Your *Sister*

Nobody *Loves You* Like Your *Sister*

New Leaf Press

First Printing: February 2004
Third Printing: May 2007

Cover by RS Walch Art & Design, Murfreesboro, TN
Interior design by Brent Spurlock
Edited by Jim Fletcher and Roger Howerton

ISBN-13: 978-0-89221-568-3
ISBN-10: 0-89221-568-2
Library of Congress Catalog Card Number: 2003116021

Printed in the United States of America.

New Leaf Press
A Division of New Leaf Publishing Group

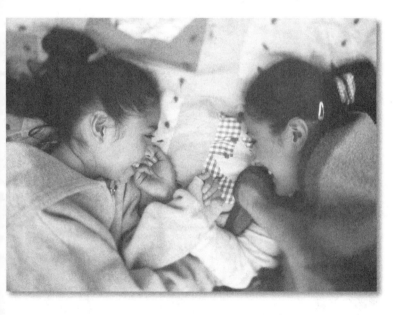

*. . . for he hath said, I will never
leave thee, nor forsake thee.*
— Hebrews 13:5

A special gift for you

To

_____

From

_____

INTRODUCTION

I t's about relationships. How many times have you
heard that? It's true, isn't it?

Life is very much tied to the relationships we have
with people: family, friends, even enemies. Unless we
live alone in a forest, we interact with other humans
on a daily basis.

And because we are human, love becomes a huge
part of our relationships. We crave it, nurture it, hope
for it. For obvious reasons, those we live with are
the recipients of varying degrees of love. A little one
approaches because someone stepped on his finger
during play-time. A phone call is about one sister
needing another sister, right now. A plea from college

gives a mom or dad the opportunity to "love on" a homesick freshman.

If life is beautiful, then love is its face. The stories and vignettes in this book are about people and their relationships with those they love. They'll make you feel good, maybe make you cry, maybe cause you to think a bit more about someone who needs you.

Even the lengths of these love reminders have been chosen with care: sometimes you need a quick pick-me-up, a short read. Sometimes you have the time, and perhaps the need, to curl up for awhile and read about the human relationship.

Wherever you are in your life journey, take time to pause and reflect. It's all about love; everything else is just noise. Because nobody loves you like your sister.

THE PAPER *Cup*

To Sis

O ne night I was sitting in my kitchen, half-listening as my 15-year-old brother Tommy antagonized my 12-year-old brother Kevin. I didn't pay attention when Kevin charged up the stairs with the hurt on his face.

About 20 minutes later, as I was walking upstairs I heard Kevin crying inside the bathroom. I bit my tongue to stop myself from saying, "Come on Kev, don't be such a baby." Instead, I knocked on the door and asked, "Hey Kev, do you wanna talk?"

No response.

I tried again, "Hey why don't you come out of there?"

Again, no response.

So, joking around, I grabbed a stack of index cards and a pencil and wrote, "If you don't want to talk, we can write notes to each other."

An hour later I was still sitting on the floor outside the bathroom with two stacks of index cards in front of me. One was blank and one was cards from Kevin on which he had translated all his yucky feelings into words for me. By this time, I didn't care about the rings of my precious phone and "Dawson's Creek" show downstairs. As I read one of Kevin's notes, tears came to my eyes. It said, "Nobody in this family cares about me. I'm not the youngest, and I'm not the oldest, and I'm not talented. Tommy thinks I'm a wuss and Dad wishes he had the other Kevin as a kid because he's better at basketball. And you're never around to even notice me."

Tears came to my eyes as I wrote back to him. It was true what he had said about me. I wrote back, "You know Kev, I really do love you and I'm sorry I don't always show it. I am here for you and you are loved in this family."

There was no response for a while, but then
I heard a tearing sound coming from inside the
bathroom. Kevin, who had run out of index cards
wrote on a torn up paper cup, "Thanks."

I wrote back "For what?" It returned to me with
"Loving me" written on it. Since then, I try my
best to never only half-notice my family members
anymore. Kevin and I have a closer relationship now,
and sometimes when one of us notices that the other
is upset we'll smile and say "Write it on a paper cup."

SISTER'S *Day*

To Sis

In the autumn of 1989, my then nine-year-old sister, LaLoni asked me a question that started a special family tradition. At 19, I was out of the house often with school, church events, dating, and hanging out with girlfriends. LaLoni and I were very close, but she felt I was spending too much time away from her. She said she missed me and asked me if we could spend the day together soon. We looked at the calendar and decided that October 5, 1989 would be a good date. In order to make the day extra special, we decided to exchange small gifts. We were both very excited; and she decided to name the day "Sister's Day." The bond of sisterhood is so special to us. We celebrated our thirteenth Sister's Day on October 5, 2002. We've added to the day's events venturing to the mall, a restaurant, the movies, a play, or a day of pampering at the hair and nail salon. A few years ago, we even scheduled a Sisters photo shoot at a local portrait studio. We had a ball! My sister is my best friend, prayer partner, and confidant. I thank

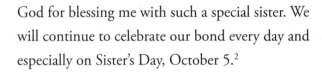

God for blessing me with such a special sister. We will continue to celebrate our bond every day and especially on Sister's Day, October 5.[2]

Be glad in the LORD and rejoice, ye righteous: and shout for joy, all ye that are upright in heart.
— Psalm 32:11

Leisure

What is this life if, full of care,
We have no time to stand and stare?
No time to stand beneath the boughs
And stare as long as sheep or cows.
No time to see, when woods we pass,

Where squirrels hide their nuts in grass.
No time to see, in broad daylight,
Streams full of stars, like skies at night.
No time to turn at Beauty's glance,
And watch her feet, how they can dance.
No time to wait till her mouth can
Enrich that smile her eyes began.
A poor life this if, full of care,
We have no time to stand and stare.[3]

Does not wisdom cry out, And understanding lift up her voice? She takes her stand on the top of the high hill, Beside the way, where the paths meet.

– Proverbs 8:1-2

TO THE *Moon*

hen I was in kindergarten, my teacher asked each child a simple question: If you were going to the moon and you could only take one thing, what would it be? Answers varied from toys to bikes and pets. My answer was simple: I would take my sister! I was five years old then and 29 years later I would answer the same way. . . . YES — I would take my sister to the moon![4]

ROLLS-ROYCE
Dreams

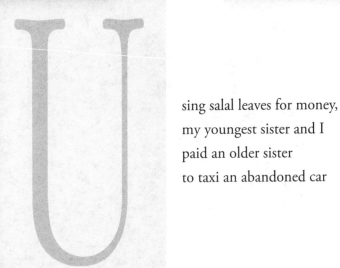

Using salal leaves for money,
my youngest sister and I
paid an older sister
to taxi an abandoned car

in our backyard. Our sister
knew how to shift gears,
turn smoothly with a hand signal,
and make perfect screeching stop sounds.
We drove to the beach,
to the market, to Sunday School,
past our would-be boyfriends' houses,
to any town, anywhere.
We shopped for expensive clothes everywhere.
Our sister would open our doors
and say, *Meter's runnin' ladies,*
but take your time.
We rode all over in that ugly green Hudson
with its broken front windshield, springs poking
through its back seat, blackberry vines growing
through rusted floorboards;

with no wheels, no tires, taillights busted,
headlights missing, and gas gauge on empty.[5]

For wisdom is better than rubies, and all things one may desire cannot be compared with her.
– Proverbs 8:11

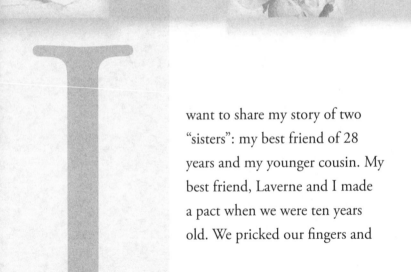

BLOOD *Sisters*

I want to share my story of two "sisters": my best friend of 28 years and my younger cousin. My best friend, Laverne and I made a pact when we were ten years old. We pricked our fingers and rubbed them together and became blood sisters from that time. She has been a great support, a wonderful friend and truly my sister. We share a bond that is lifelong. My cousin, Tracy is ten years younger than me and since the day she was born, I watched over her. She has grown up to be an incredible woman, a great wife and a wonderful mother. I love them both dearly![1]

> *"The family you come from isn't as important as the family you're going to have."*
>
> – Ring Lardner

> *Pleasant words are like a honeycomb, Sweetness to the soul and health to the bones.*
>
> – Proverbs 16:24

Listening

L istening is a magnetic and strange thing, a creative force. The friends who listen to us are the ones we

move toward, and we want to sit in their
radius. When we are listened to, it
creates us, makes us unfold and expand.[6]

And though I bestow all my goods to feed the poor, and though
I give my body to be burned, but have not love, it profits me
nothing.
                                                            – I Corinthians 13:3

MY *Second* F ATHER

M

y father died when I was five. It
was hard on us all. With time the
wounds healed. My brother, who
is eight years older than I, began
to watch over my mother and me.

Taking on many more responsibilities than were expected of him, I remember he made sure the trash was taken out, and the yard mowed. He did this on his own, without being told to do so.

Because of my father's death, my mother was forced to get a full time job. My brother took it upon himself to get up early every morning. He would get me up for school, and make me breakfast. While I was eating he would lay out my clothes, make my bed, and gather my school books up.

Hand in hand we would walk to the bus stop. As we waited, he would play games my father used to play with me. He did his best to make me happy, and he succeeded every time.

When we arrived home from school, we were alone for about a half hour, until Mom got home from work. He would sit me down with three cookies and a glass of milk. If I had homework, then this was the time I would do it. My brother would start laundry, and do dishes if there were any. He would find something for supper, and have everything ready for Mom, so she could start cooking.

Mom would greet us with a hug and kiss. This was our cue to go outside and have some fun. This was my brother's time to be a kid.

It was a Saturday in June a couple years later. My mother and I were at the store. They had the Father's Day cards out. I stared at the rack of cards. My mom said "Honey, I know this is a hard time for you."

I said, "No, Mom that's not it. Why don't they have Brother's Day cards?"

She smiled and said, "You're right; your brother has definitely been a father to you. Go ahead. Pick out a card."

So I did, and on Father's Day, my mother and I sat my brother down and gave him the card.

As he read it, I saw the tears forming in his eyes. I felt a lump in my throat, as he threw his arms around me and my mother. I heard the crackling in mom's voice as she said, "Son, your father is proud of you, seeing that he raised a good man, and that you do your best to fill his shoes. We love you, and thank you." [7]

Duty done is the soul's fireside.
– Robert Browning

A LESSON *Learned*

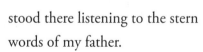

I stood there listening to the stern words of my father.

He had gathered us into our enclosed patio and had the

look on his face that told us all that one of us did something wrong.

"Which one of you did this?" he asked with a sharp voice.

We all stared down at the floor containing the art of a child's handwriting in chalk. I suppose that had been a no-no for us, though I can't say I quite remember that part when I was committing this horrible crime.

I stood there, trembling on the inside and had hoped that no one else could see it. Will he know it was me? I secretly wondered. Scared, the only words that came from my mouth were, "Not me, Dad."

The others denied it as well. Of course, we knew that one of us must have done it. But I, being the youngest and smallest of the three, just couldn't find the courage to tell the truth. It wasn't that I was a bad kid. Lying was not normal for me. But the look on my dad's face that evening sent a chill up and down my spine and somehow I couldn't bring myself to tell him.

He had a way about him when I was a child that made me afraid of him. But I loved him for it too, because it gave me my limits, my boundaries of what I could and could not do. I wanted to please him, of course. Maybe that's why I held back the truth that day. I was afraid of displeasing the one man I looked up to.

Without saying a word, he disappeared for only minutes and came back with a piece of paper and a pencil. He was so determined to find the culprit!

"I want each of you to write exactly what you see on the step." I was not a stupid kid, though and when my

turn came, I deliberately wrote the words differently. So when my dad compared the handwriting, he still couldn't tell which one of us did it.

Frustrated, he stood a step above us and looked down at his three small kids.

"I'm going to give you one more chance to confess."

He continued to stand there for a few moments, but to me it only seemed like a second. Not surprisingly, neither my brother nor my sister spoke up. Why should they? I was the one who did it. Should I say something? Is it too late? He'll be mad! So again, frightened, I held my tongue.

"Well, if someone would have come forward when I asked, there would have been no punishment." Oh, no! I've lost my chance! "But now it's too late." Stupid, stupid, stupid! I should have confessed! Now

I'm gonna get it!

He took us all in the house as tears welled up in my eyes.

"Since none of you seemed to have done it, then you all get a spanking." What?! Still, I stood there and said nothing. The last thing I wanted was a spanking!

"I did it," someone said and I was pretty sure it wasn't me.

I looked around to see my sister come forward. Huh? She did it? No, she didn't because I did. Why was she taking the blame for something I did? Feeling guilty, yet still scared to 'fess up, I stood there knowing my sister was going to get spanked for something I did. And I let it happen. I didn't speak up.

We didn't talk about that day for many years. Not until we were all older and I knew it was safe to finally tell my dad it was really me. By that time, I had already figured out why my sister took the rap for it. She had become my protector, my worry-wort, my best friend. And because of that, she would have rather taken the pain herself than see me suffer.

We joke about it now — all of us, including my sister. And as I always felt guilty because of it, that was the last time I let anyone take the blame for me.

When I think back to that day, I know I learned the value of family, of a sister who would do anything for me. And I'm glad to say that I know now I would do the same for her.[8]

> *Those who do not love their fellow human beings live unfruitful lives.*
>
> – Percy Bysshe Shelley

THE *Home* RUN

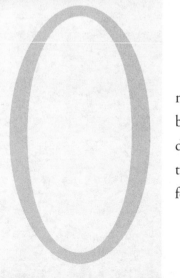

On June 18th, I went to my little brother's baseball game as I always did. Cory was 12 years old at the time and had been playing baseball for a couple of years. When I saw that he was warming up to be next at bat, I decided to head over to the dugout to give him a few pointers. But when I got there, I simply said, "I love you."

In return, he asked, "Does this mean you want me to hit a home run?"

I smiled and said, "Do your best."

As he walked up to the plate, there was a certain aura about him. He looked so confident and so sure about what he was going to do. One swing was all he took and, wouldn't you know, he hit his first home run! He ran around those bases with such pride — his eyes sparkled and his face was lit up. But what touched my heart the most was when he walked back over to the dugout. He looked over at me with the biggest smile I've ever seen and said, "I love you too, Ter."

I don't remember if his team won or lost that game. On that special summer day in June, it simply didn't matter.[9]

When the woman whose son was living spoke to the king, for she yearned with compassion for her son; and she said, "O my lord, give her the living child, and by no means kill him!" But the other said, "Let him be neither mine nor yours, but divide him." So the king answered and said, "Give the first woman the living child, and by no means kill him; she is the mother."

– I Kings 3:26-27

Love feels no burden,
thinks nothing of trouble,
attempts what is above its strength,
pleads no excuse of impossibility;
for it thinks all things lawful for
itself, and all things possible.
It is therefore able to undertake all things,
and warrants them to take effect,
where he who does not love,
would faint and lie down.

– Thomas A Kempis

> *Do you see a man who excels in his work?*
> *He will stand before kings; He will not*
> *stand before unknown men.*
> — Proverbs 22:29

EIGHT DAYS
Before CHRISTMAS

hen did my life begin? In all truth I would have to say that it began eight days before Christmas when I was already the mature age of nine years old. Or to be more exact, I was nine and a half. That extra half makes all the difference in the world to a child who wants to grow up quickly. December 17, 1986, that is the day I so vividly remember. My mind is a VCR that can play, rewind, fast forward, and pause any second of that day. But regretfully, I cannot stop it.

Oh yes, it started out just like any regular day for a young boy just itching to get out of school as quickly as possible. I was always the teacher's pet and the quiet type, but just between you and me, school was no roller coaster ride. The most terrifying thing I remember is my teacher from that year. Oh how I would dread the end of the school day. Miss Tanner would stand by the door as we filed out one by one and kiss us on the cheek. It was a slobbering mess.

I cannot recall what the weather was like that day — it seems like such a trite and needless detail. But I can tell you this much: we lived in South Florida, so I can pretty much guarantee you that it was hot. The sky may have been blue but your skin would be bright red. No, I don't remember what the weather was like, but I do know that it couldn't have been beautiful.

I would meet my sister, Sarah, at the bike racks as soon as school let out. She was two years younger than I and probably a lot prettier. We lived nearly two miles from the school grounds and had driven our bikes to and from the campus all year. We walked the distance before that year because there were no sidewalks along the side of the road leading to our home. Our parents both worked full time and riding our bikes back and forth wasn't exactly a hardship, it was more like a grown-up responsibility. More importantly, it was fun.

Now you have to understand, we needed to get

home as quickly as possible. With Christmas being so close, we assured ourselves that there were possibly unwrapped presents lying around hidden in our parents' room. The goal was to get home before Mom and Dad. My sister and I were cohorts in this great and terrible deed. Pssst, it wasn't the first time.

Anyway, we rode like mad, passing by tons of new houses going up in our developing city. New hotels and supermarkets were arriving nearly every day. There were many times we saw a tour bus drive by slowly filled with people eager to spend every penny they had. On what, I have no idea. Royal Palm Beach was just a speck becoming a star at the time.

A smiling crossing guard led us silently across the last intersection before our intended destination. Just four more blocks and we waited side by side for the traffic to subside before crossing the street to the dirt road our house was on. Two more minutes and we might have to chance to sneak a peek at our presents.

I don't know which way my eyes were looking but I did see the white van. It was the last vehicle that would pass us before we crossed the street. I looked over at Sarah. Her eyes were focused on something down the road in the opposite direction. That's when I realized that her feet were propelling her bike forward.

"Sarah, No!" I screamed at the top of my lungs. She was in the opposite lane, almost across the street. Screeching tires. My sister never turned her head. I watched her fly off of her bike and skid several feet along the harsh pavement.

"Sarah! Sarah!"

The driver of the white van jumped out quickly. He slammed the door shut and pressed his body against the side of his vehicle. He pounded his fists furiously against it. I looked at my sister lying there helplessly. There was no movement.

"I'm going to get my parents!" I shouted at the driver, not knowing what I should do or say. He glanced at me but said nothing. I ran down that old dirt road faster than a cheetah could dare ever hope for. All the while I was shouting, "Mom, Dad! Mom, Dad!" Our house was the fifth one on the right. It was a small, prefabricated home sitting on a large hill on two acres with a nice pond in the front.

I could see the front door open from halfway down the street. My mother had a hand over her chest.

"Sarah got run over! Sarah got run over!" My mother bounded furiously down the steps and ran down that road faster in flip-flops — much faster than I had in my tennis shoes. She never once looked at me or anything else on her desperate journey. Her sights were only set on keeping her daughter alive.

I continued to run all the way to our house. My father stood there looming in the hallway. I couldn't understand why he just stood there. I told him again that his daughter had been run over. He walked slowly to the phone and started dialing. He only dialed one number before asking, "This is a joke, isn't it?"

A neighbor took me over to her house only a few moments later. My father disappeared to join my mother. I wanted so badly to know what was going on. I deserved to be with my sister. She was my best friend. A friend of my mother's picked me up nearly thirty minutes later. She had a daughter that was my age that was a friend of my sister and I.

At their house I watched the movie *Never Ending Story* nearly all the way through. I spent most of the time crying by myself though. It was then that Mrs. Cramer came to me and said it was time to go home. She looked tired and her daughter was crying hysterically. I was only confused. No one told me anything. I just wanted to see my sister and make sure she was going to be okay. She was going to be just fine; I never doubted that for one minute.

Mrs. Cramer stopped the car halfway down the driveway and told her daughter to go pick a rose from the rosebushes in their front yard. She only cried more as she did so.

When we finally got back to my house there were people everywhere. Friends, neighbors, family, and police. My father grabbed me by the shoulders and led me to an old wooden swing just in front of the house. He sat beside me and without any fanfare or explanation he said, "Tim, your sister is dead."

Yes, that is the day my life began, eight days before Christmas. It changed the way I feel about people and events. Christmas presents aren't the most important things in life — family and friends are. I cherish and respect every living day. I learned early on that you must let the ones you love know that you love them. Thirteen years later I still cry when I think about my sister and that terrible day. I don't remember much about her and I can't even picture what she looks like in my mind. But I do know this; I know I loved her.[10]

Weep not for me, but for yourselves.
— John Bunyan

If the clouds are full of rain, They empty themselves upon the earth; And if a tree falls to the south or the north, In the place where the tree falls, there it shall lie.
— Ecclesiastes 11:3

CHEERING ME On

I close my eyes as tight as they can go.

The lights go off, and my imagination switches on. Pictures flash through my mind like an old film from the fifties.

I remember driving home by myself for the first time. Now, I look into the future and imagine that I am walking across the stage to receive my college diploma. The years pass, and I hear my fiancé say "I do." I look further and listen to the gentle gurgles coming from my baby's nursery. A smile discreetly appears as memories past and thoughts of the future travel through my soul.

I journey to memories of my high school graduation, and a tear suddenly trickles down my cheek. I look into the bleachers packed with families and friends. I see my parents wrapped in pride, and I look to their side for Katie and Kevin's approval. But Katie, my older sister, is not there.

My eyes abruptly open as I am snapped back into reality. I remember being called out of Spanish class in tenth grade and taken to the hospital to see

Katie, who had cancer, for the final time. It was an excruciating task, but I found the good in Katie's tragic death.

Katie's room is exactly the way she left it on a Friday night in September, 1993, when she was carried to the ambulance on a stretcher. Her James Dean poster hangs on one wall; her elementary school track ribbons and collection of porcelain masks hangs on the others. Her bed is neatly made and lined with stuffed animals — typical of a girl who would visit her sloppier friends and, without prompting, start vacuuming their rooms.

Katie died just a few weeks into her freshman year at the University of Miami. At eighteen she was 5'5" tall and had straight shoulder-length blond hair, big blue eyes, and pale, clear skin. Her senior year in high school, Katie was the varsity cheerleader captain and valedictorian.

More importantly, though, she was my best friend. After all, when she was six years old, she had declared herself old enough to take care of her little sister and brand new baby brother, because she thought our mother was not sharing us enough with her. This caring attitude continued throughout her life. Katie would always braid my hair, go shopping with me, and let me go out with her and her friends when I was lonely and bored. Katie would always tutor Kevin, who has a learning disability, when he needed help with his homework. She would continually drill him on his studies until he got it right. Afterward, she would take him to go get ice cream as a reward. Clearly, Katie was not just our older sister. She was also our teacher, friend, and second mother.

Katie always surrounded herself with friends. She was constantly opening her ears, heart, and arms to someone in need. The phone was constantly ringing and her room was always crowded with people in it. Now, my house is silent.

I realize that getting caught in a pool of depression only leads to drowning. I live by looking for the positive in the worst situations. I now have a relationship with my parents and brother that means everything to me. I know what is important in life, and it is not always partying and getting A's. But most of all, I know that I can handle anything. Life is not easy, but I overcame one of its toughest obstacles.

I believe the hardest part of death is the experiences it steals. Katie will not be clapping for me when I finally get my college diploma or giving me advice on my wedding day. My children will only hear stories of the girlhood of their aunt, both stories of reality and an imagined future.

I close my eyes as tight as they can go.

A diploma is placed in my hand. "I do" echoes from a distance. Katie says she loves me and hugs me tight on a September afternoon in 1993. Just before I cross my high school auditorium stage, I look out at the spectators in the bleachers, and I see Mother and Father and Kevin.

Katie is sitting right beside them, cheering me on.[11]

For behold, I create new heavens and a new earth; And the former shall not be remembered or come to mind.
— Isaiah 65:17

Yes, JESUS LOVES ME

Anna and her sister Susan Warner lived near the West Point Military base. They had the privilege of seeing many young servicemen come to know Jesus. They would conduct weekly Bible school classes for the men. After their father died, Susan started writing some fiction novels. One that she wrote in 1860 was entitled "Say and Seal." In it a poem was needed to give comfort to a dying child, so Susan's sister Anna wrote the words, "Jesus Loves Me." In 1861, Dr. William Bradbury wrote the tune and added the chorus to this hymn that children around the world sing.

Christianity demands a level of caring that transcends human inclinations.

– Erwin Lutzer

Jesus loves me! This I know, for the Bible tells me so;

Little ones to Him belong; They are weak but He is strong.

Jesus loves me! He who died, Heaven's gate to open wide;

He will wash away my sin, let His little child come in.

Jesus loves me! He will stay close beside me all the way;

Thou hast bled and died for me,

I will henceforth live for thee.

Yes, Jesus loves me!

Yes, Jesus loves me!

Yes, Jesus loves me! The Bible tells me so.

And he looked up and saw the rich putting their gifts into the treasury. And he saw also a certain poor widow putting in two mites. So He said, "Truly I say to you that this poor widow has put in more than all; for all these out of their abundance have put in offerings for God, but she out of her poverty put in all the livelihood that she had."
– Luke 21:1-4

THE *Richest* FAMILY IN TOWN

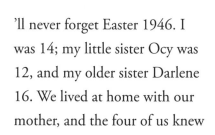

I'll never forget Easter 1946. I was 14; my little sister Ocy was 12, and my older sister Darlene 16. We lived at home with our mother, and the four of us knew what it was to do without many things. My dad had died five years before, leaving Mom with seven school kids to raise and no money. By 1946, my older sisters were married and my brothers had left home.

A month before Easter, the pastor of our church announced that a special Easter offering would be taken to help a poor family. He asked everyone to save and give sacrificially.

When we got home, we talked about what we could do. We decided to buy 50 pounds of potatoes and live on them for a month. This would allow us to save 20 dollars of our grocery money for the offering. Then we thought that if we kept our electric lights turned out as much as possible and didn't listen to the radio, we'd save money on that month's electric bill. Darlene got as many house and yard cleaning jobs as possible, and both of us babysat for everyone we could. For 15 cents we could buy enough cotton loops to make potholders to sell three for one dollar. We made 20 dollars on potholders.

That month was one of the best of our lives.

Every day we counted the money to see how much we had saved. At night we'd sit in the dark and talk about how the poor family was going to enjoy having the money the church would give them. We had about 80 people in church, so we figured that whatever amount of money we had to give, the offering would surely be 20 times that much. After all, every Sunday the pastor had reminded everyone to save for the sacrificial offering.

The day before Easter, Ocy and I walked to the grocery store and got the manager to give us three crisp 20-dollar bills and one 10-dollar bill for all our change. We ran all the way home to show Mom and Darlene. We had never had so much money before. That night we were so excited we could hardly sleep. We didn't care that we wouldn't have new clothes for Easter; we had 70 dollars for the sacrificial offering.

We could hardly wait to get to church! On Sunday morning, rain was pouring. We didn't own an umbrella, and the church was over a mile from our home, but it didn't seem to matter how wet we got. Darlene had cardboard in her shoes to fill the holes. The cardboard came apart, and her feet got wet.

But we sat in church proudly. I heard some teenagers talking about the Smith girls having on their old dresses. I looked at them in their new clothes, and I felt rich.

When the sacrificial offering was taken, we were

sitting on the second row from the front. Mom put in the ten-dollar bill, and each of us kids put in a twenty. As we walked home after church, we sang all the way. At lunch Mom had a surprise for us. She had bought a dozen eggs, and we had boiled Easter eggs with our fried potatoes!

Late that afternoon the minister drove up in his car. Mom went to the door, talked with him for a moment, and then came back with an envelope in her hand. We asked what it was, but she didn't say a word. She opened the envelope and out fell a bunch of money. There were three crisp 20-dollar bills, one ten-dollar bill, and seventeen one-dollar bills.

Mom put the money back in the envelope. We didn't talk; we just sat and stared at the floor. We had gone from feeling like millionaires to feeling like poor

white trash. We kids had such a happy life that we felt
sorry for anyone who didn't have our Mom and Dad
for parents and a house full of brothers and sisters and
other kids visiting constantly. We thought it was fun
to share silverware and see whether we got the spoon
or the fork that night. We had two knives that we
passed around to whoever needed them. I knew we
didn't have a lot of things that other people had, but
I had never thought we were poor. That Easter day I
found out we were.

The minister had brought *us* the money for the
poor family, so we must be poor. I didn't like being
poor. I looked at my dress and worn-out shoes and felt
so ashamed. I didn't even want to go back to church.
Everyone there probably already knew we were poor.

I thought about school. I was in the ninth grade

and at the top of my class of over 100 students. I wondered if the kids at school knew that we were poor. I decided that I could quit school since I had finished the eighth grade. That was all the law required at that time. We sat in silence for a long time. Then it got dark, and we went to bed.

All that week, we girls went to school and came home, and no one talked much. Finally on Saturday, Mom asked us that we wanted to do with the money. What did poor people do with money? We didn't know. We'd never known we were poor.

We didn't want to go to church on Sunday, but Mom said we had to. Although it was a sunny day, we didn't talk on the way. Mom started to sing, but no one joined in and she only sang one verse.

At church we had a missionary speaker. He talked about how churches in Africa made buildings out of sun-dried bricks, but they needed money to buy roofs. He said 100 dollars would put a roof on a church.

The minister said, "Can't we all sacrifice to help these poor people?" We looked at each other and smiled for the first time in a week. Mom reached into her purse and pulled out the envelope. She passed it to Darlene. Darlene gave it to me, and I handed it to Ocy. Ocy put it in the offering.

When the offering was counted, the minister announced that it was a little over 100 dollars. The missionary was excited. He hadn't expected such a large offering from our small church.

He said, "You must have some rich people in this church."

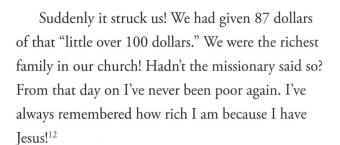

Suddenly it struck us! We had given 87 dollars of that "little over 100 dollars." We were the richest family in our church! Hadn't the missionary said so? From that day on I've never been poor again. I've always remembered how rich I am because I have Jesus![12]

Never interfere with God's providential dealings with other souls. Be true to God yourself and watch.
— Oswald Chambers

> *Blessed are you poor, For yours is the kingdom of God.*
>
> – Luke 6:20

Devoted SISTERS

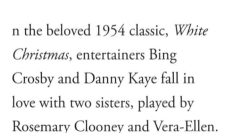

In the beloved 1954 classic, *White Christmas*, entertainers Bing Crosby and Danny Kaye fall in love with two sisters, played by Rosemary Clooney and Vera-Ellen.

The ladies' famous number "Sisters" was a highlight of the film; the Irving Berlin composition featured the dancing and singing skills of these two talented actresses, and is remembered as an ode to the bond of sisterhood. Enjoy!

Sisters

isters, sisters

There were never such devoted sisters;

Never had to have a chaperone, no sir,

I'm there to keep my eye on her.

Caring, sharing

Every little thing that we are wearing;
When a certain gentleman arrived from Rome,
She wore the dress, and I stayed home.
All kinds of weather, we stick together,
The same in the rain and sun;
Two different faces, but in tight places,
We think and we act as one.
Those who've seen us
Know that not a thing could come between us;
Many men have tried to split us up, but no one can.
Lord help the mister who comes between me and my sister,
And Lord help the sister who comes between me and
my man.[13]

ALL *Gummed* UP

One of our favorite dishes at home when I was growing up was Mother's special fried eggplant.

My older sister, Virginia, had a boyfriend, Clifford, who worked through the evening, then often stopped over while Virginia fixed him a late supper.

One evening she was frying some eggplant slices, just like Mama made, when I happened along. It had been a while since dinner, and when Virginia turned her back, I filched a couple of cooked slices and began to eat my ill-gotten treat.

Just as I finished the first slice, I considered what might happen when Virginia noticed my theft, so I quietly slipped the remaining slice from my plate back into the frying pan.

All would have gone well if not for the piece of Juicy Fruit gum that I'd parked on my plate. It had been slipped into the skillet with that slice I returned, and now every piece of eggplant became saturated with the melted aromatic gum.

I always wondered if that's why Virginia and Clifford never married.[14]

Best FRIENDS

here are as many definitions of sister as there are, well, sisters. Big or small, one or more, each relationship is as different as that sister is to you.

There is no relationship like that with a sister. She can be either the comforting hand that held yours as you rode the bus for the first time, or the rude kick in the pants that leaves you sprawling face first in the mud. Or she might have always been good for a laugh when she would start screaming after she found that frog you hid as a surprise in her little pink shoes.

She is either that annoying person who seems to have moved into the bathroom full time, or the one that laughingly doesn't mind if you tag along when she is going somewhere, or she just might be both depending on what day it is and just how aggravating you have been lately. Your sister either captured your heart that day as a newborn when she first smiled at you, and you finally had someone smaller than you to cherish, annoy, or compete with. Or she is the person you most wanted to be when you grew up. She might be the one person that you can talk to when your world falls apart, or she is the one person that gets on your nerves faster than anyone else on the planet when you least expect it, usually on holidays and over stuff that is trivial like cranberry sauce salad.

Regardless, she is your sister – and that makes her a very special person in your life. Nobody can make you laugh, cry, smile, scream, and feel loved like she can. And as time passes, it is a relationship that can become even more precious with shared youth, shared memories, and shared loss. She became your sister by chance, but she is your greatest fan and your best friend by choice.

You can kid the world. But not your sister.
– Charlotte Gray

Open rebuke is better than love carefully concealed.
– Proverbs 27:5

Miracle OF GOD'S LOVE

S ubject: You are my sunshine!!!

"You are my sunshine, my only sunshine"

Like any good mother, when Karen found out that another baby was on the way, she did what she could to help her three-year-old son Michael prepare for a new sibling. They found out that the new baby was going be a girl, and day after day, night after night, Michael sang to his sister in Mommy's tummy. He was building a bond of love with his little sister before he even met her.

The pregnancy progressed normally for Karen, an active member of the Panther Creek United Methodist Church in Morristown, Tennessee.

In time, the labor pains came. Soon it was every five minutes, every three, every minute. But serious complications arose during delivery and Karen found herself in hours of labor. Would a C-section be required?

Finally, after a long struggle, Michael's little sister

was born, but she was in very serious condition. With a siren howling in the night, the ambulance rushed the infant to the neonatal intensive care unit at St. Mary's Hospital, Knoxville, Tennessee.

The days inched by. The little girl got worse. The pediatrician had to tell the parents there is very little hope. Be prepared for the worst.

Karen and her husband contacted a local cemetery about a burial plot. They had fixed up a special room in their house for their new baby but now they found themselves having to plan for a funeral. Michael, however, kept begging his parents to let him see his sister. "I want to sing to her," he kept saying.

Week two in intensive care looked as if a funeral would come before the week was over. Michael kept nagging about singing to his sister, but kids are never allowed in intensive care. Karen decided to take

Michael whether they liked it or not. If he didn't see his sister right then, he may never see her alive.

She dressed him in an oversized scrub suit and marched him into ICU. He looked like a walking laundry basket.

The head nurse recognized him as a child and bellowed, "Get that kid out of here now. No children are allowed."

The mother rose up strong in Karen, and the usually mild-mannered lady glared steel-eyed right into the head nurse's face, her lips a firm line. "He is not leaving until he sings to his sister," she stated. Then Karen towed Michael to his sister's bedside.

He gazed at the tiny infant losing the battle to live.

After a moment, he began to sing. In the pure-hearted voice of a three-year-old, Michael sang: "You are my sunshine, my only sunshine; you make me happy when skies are gray."

Instantly the baby girl seemed to respond. The pulse rate began to calm down and become steady. Mother stood with tears in her eyes.

"You never know, dear, how much I love you, please don't take my sunshine away."

As Michael sang to his sister, the baby's ragged, strained breathing became as smooth as a kitten's purr. "Keep on singing, sweetheart."

"The other night, dear, as I lay sleeping, I dreamed I held you in my arms."

Michael's little sister began to relax as rest, healing rest, seemed to sweep over her. "Keep on singing, Michael."

Tears had now conquered the face of the bossy head nurse. Karen glowed.

"You are my sunshine, my only sunshine. Please don't take my sunshine away. . . ."

The next day . . . the very next day . . . the little girl was well enough to go home.

Woman's Day magazine called it "The Miracle of a Brother's Song."

The medical staff just called it a miracle.

Karen called it a miracle of God's love.

A sister is a little bit of childhood that can never be lost.

– Marion C. Garretty

The blind see and the lame walk; the lepers are cleansed and the deaf hear; the dead are raised up and the poor have the gospel preached to them.

– Matthew 11:5

THE *Gift*

I was looking through some old
photo albums when I came
across the newspaper clippings
and pictures I'd somehow put

in the back of my mind. The headline jumped out at me. "New Kidney, New Life for Boy." I reread the story that had made the front page of the newspaper. . . . a story of a nightmare that I had lived through somehow.

It was the winter of 1979 in Michigan. I had been casually following TV news reports about an illness called Reye's syndrome that had been hitting area children. I was a stay-at-home mom of a two-year-old son. My sister lived only four miles from me and we would chat on the phone daily about our kids and just life in general. She told me that Paul had a sore throat and was staying home from school that week. Paul seemed to feel better on Friday and when my sister asked if he was ready to go back to school, he said he didn't think so because he had heard on television that kids were getting really sick from some syndrome and he thought he'd best stay home one more day. Shirley, my sister, didn't push it and let him stay home.

The next morning, my sister awoke with severe chest pains. Russ, her husband, was going to take her to the emergency room. Paul helped tie her shoes for her as it hurt for her to bend over with what turned out to be a collapsed lung. She was admitted to the hospital and everyone's focus was on her for the time being. Paul seemed to relapse from his sore throat and had begun vomiting. A call to his pediatrician resulted in a prescription for some nausea medicine being prescribed. He was sleeping a lot and everyone figured he must have a virus or a flu bug. Russ had his hands full. His wife was in one hospital with a collapsed lung. His child was sick at home, and he had gotten a call to rush his own father to another hospital for a possible brain tumor. He was juggling running back and forth trying to tend to all these serious situations.

I had just sent my husband off to work and got my son down for a nap when the phone rang. It was my brother-in-law calling from the hospital. Paul had now been admitted and the diagnosis was Reye's syndrome. I hung up and felt a terrible panic. All the news reports came flooding back to me and I knew this was a grave diagnosis for my little 12-year-old nephew.

When I arrived I went to my sister's room and we were all upset and in a panic for what to do. All of us went into a conference room with a team of doctors who tried to explain the situation concerning Paul and what their plan of operation was to be. He was to stay here in the intensive care unit and they would be in touch by phone with the specialist at Children's Hospital for the night. The staff had agreed to let my sister visit her son in the intensive care unit. She was on oxygen and IVs but I managed to get her into a wheel chair and into the elevator. The staff nurse on duty kindly showed us the way to where Paul was at. The curtain was pulled from around his bed and the reality of how gravely ill he was set in.

He was in a coma but his eyes were partially open. . . . but not seeing. A tear or two would fall down his cheek, but it was explained that he was not crying. He was unconscious. He had stopped breathing on his own and was on a ventilator. The heaving and hissing of the machine took over the silence of the room. I helped my sister up so she could get close to him. We tried to talk to him through choked tears.

Tears were streaming down my sister's face and my heart broke for her. We just stood there and cried and hugged each other. There was nothing we could do but pray as it seemed Paul was in God's hands now. It was decided by the doctors finally that Paul was to be transported to Children's Hospital. As I left to take my sister back to her room, the nurse handed me Paul's bag of clothes to take with me. I don't know why, but holding that bag made me feel like I was holding the last of Paul in my hands. I clutched it tightly when I was alone and cried and cried.

I stayed at the hospital with my sister day and night. Rules were broken and I was allowed to stay in the bed next to her along with her other son, Rusty, who was 15. Sis and I would turn on the television news to catch the reports about Paul as it was being covered by all media. We called constantly down to Children's Hospital for any news of improvement, but there was none.

Finally, my sister was allowed to leave the hospital and I took her home with me. I picked up the two younger girls and brought them to my house as well. Sis was still not well and all the stress and strain of everything was not helping. The phone rang constantly with friends and family wanting the latest updates. There was so much chaos and confusion. I had to find some way to have quiet time to explain to the girls exactly what was happening. I also needed to help my sister try to get some rest. I was very worried about her.

I let out the sofa bed in the family room for Sis and I to sleep on. It had been many, many years since we had slept together. It was like going back into my childhood and we talked and talked way into the night about everything. We reminisced about how I used to tickle and scratch her back while she would tell me a story. We laughed and we cried and we hugged. We were two sisters bonded in grief and huddled together for comfort and had finally started to drift off to sleep. We hadn't been sleeping long before the doorbell rang. It was other family members who had come for my sister to go down to the hospital. A scan had been done and it was determined that Paul was brain dead and they were going to turn off the respirator. Decisions had to be made. . . and goodbyes said. I helped her get dressed and hugged her good-bye and I stayed with the girls.

I managed to get down to the hospital to see Paul one last time. I talked to him and promised him everything if he'd just wake up. I hoped he could hear us all talking to him. It was his mother's birthday. I didn't want him to die on his mother's birthday.

The plug was pulled and his organs were harvested and donated, as was requested by my sister and her husband. The funeral was a few days later . . . on his father's birthday. A large crowd of people came and the funeral home was packed. Flowers were everywhere. Grown men bawled like babies. Children hesitantly walked to the casket of their friend to say goodbye. Paul's teachers and principal had come to pay their last respects. It was the worst thing I think I

ever had to endure, but we got through it somehow.
Paul was plucked suddenly from our lives, but was
now in God's hands.

A letter from the hospital came to my sister. The
letter was to let her know that Paul's organs had been
donated and thanking her. The recipient of one of
Paul's kidneys was a little boy named Rocky. He was
ten years old and had suffered kidney failure following
a mysterious two-month coma. He'd been sick for
two years. He was dying and so weak he was confined
to a wheelchair. He had been in the hospital at the
same time as Paul just down the hall. His parents
got the call that a kidney was available. . . . Paul's
kidney. Rocky's parents had read about Paul's death,
one of four Reye's syndrome fatalities, in a Detroit
newspaper. Rocky had a chance now of having a

normal life again. The story of the transplant and donor was printed in the newspaper. The clipping is now yellow with age in my photo album. It was a story of the greatest gift of all. . . one that was paid for with many tears for our dear Paul.

On the one-year anniversary of Paul's death, my sister got a letter in the mail. It was from Rocky's mom. She explained that Rocky said a prayer every day for her and for Paul, and how grateful he is to be alive. He had recovered, and the kidney he had received was working. He was out of the wheelchair and able to go back to school. He was feeling the best he had in two years. This precious child had been given a gift of a new kidney and another chance to live. His parent's joy must have been tremendous. One family's loss was another family's answer to a prayer. I think we all took some comfort in knowing that a part of Paul was alive and that his death was not in vain. The loss had a purpose. His death had been a gift to Rocky.

Paul would now be a grown man 37 years of age. One wonders what his life would have been like. It's hard to imagine as he will always be 12 in our minds and hearts. He was freckle-faced and small for his age. He was a determined child who when he got something in his mind, he usually did it. Like saving 23 dollars in just two weeks to buy special wheels for his new disco roller skates. His father used to say he was "born running." He often bought tiny ceramic figures from rummage sales to add to his mother's collection. His father was quoted in the newspaper article as saying, "He crowded a lot into those 12 years. It's funny that Paul was the rowdiest of all the children. He needed more love than the others. I only hope I gave him enough." They are together now, as his father died 13 years later.

Celebrate the gift of life. It's cost cannot be measured. There is no debt as it is already paid for in tears.[15]

Hereby perceive we the love of God, because he laid down his life for us: and we ought to lay down our lives for the brethren.

– 1 John 3:16

AN INDESCRIBABLE *Joy*

hen 14-year-old Joe learned that his mom was pregnant, he was mortified. He wanted nothing to do with a baby sister. . . .

"Isn't it funny how the things we resist most can turn out to be

the greatest gifts of all?" Liz Mayer asks in her story
from *Chicken Soup for the Sister's Soul*, originally titled,
"Falling in Love with Molly." She writes:

> By the time our daughter, Molly, was due to
> be born, I'd grown accustomed to my 14-year-old
> son Joe's embarrassment and animosity about my
> pregnancy.
>
> I'd grown accustomed to a lot of things, not
> the least of which was having an unexpected child
> at 39, long after we thought our family of two
> boys was complete. My husband, to his eternal
> credit, was delighted. Our younger son, 11-year-
> old Shea, had keenly followed his little sister's in-
> utero development, but Joe rarely even spoke to
> me, except to say, after a marathon baby-naming
> conference, "Molly is Ron's dog's name."

When Molly arrived — tiny, quiet and perfect — her family's arms were there to draw her close. Except for Joe's, which remained crossed over his chest. It was an effort to step outside of my bliss, to beckon him into our circle of adoration. Shaking his head, he backed out of the room.

Joe arranged to be at a friend's house when Molly and I came home. He returned ten days later, just as I was coming back from Molly's first checkup. Tears streaming down my face, I sobbed, "The doctor thinks she may have a hearing problem."

As my husband soothed me, I noticed that Joe had stopped beside the baby, sound asleep in her car seat. He reached out to her, shifting her away from a bump in the carpet. "She's okay," he said. "There's nothing wrong with her. She's just little."

Three months later, after walking the floor at

four a.m. with a fretful, inconsolable (and otherwise perfectly healthy) baby, I stumbled into Joe's room. "Joe, could you take her? Dad's at work, and I really need a break."

Joe threw off his covers and took his sister from me. He laid her on his bed, tightly rewrapping her blanket. Putting her over his shoulder, he patted her back and spoke to her softly, slowly walking her up and down the hall.

Before Molly was born, a lot of people told us about the pleasures of a baby who comes late. "We had one of those," said an old gentleman. "Best thing that ever happened to us."

They assured us we'd cherish this unexpected detour in our lives. What they didn't mention was the bonus: the sight of a stroller parked by the backyard basketball net, a one-year-old shrieking in delight as lanky teenagers tore back and forth in front of her; a toddler, dressed in a hockey jersey scooping up the puck that always slid directly into her oversized glove; the two-year-old "helping" with 11th grade math; the four-year-old wrapped tightly around the legs of the smiling graduate.

No one predicted the first family visit to a college dorm, where 16 drawings of the same two stick figures competed with the air-brushed calendar girls on the wall. They didn't mention the newly muscled arms holding up a struggling swimmer, a shaky skater. They didn't prepare me for the Christmas Eve, when a seven-year-old with a brother on the other side of the world asked if she could trade all the presents under the tree for "our Joey at the door."

No one ever told me about the joy of seeing our little girl perched on the shoulders of our grown-up son, his grinning, handsome face turned up toward her laughter. They couldn't have told me, because a joy like that is indescribable.[16]

> *For when three sisters love each other with such sincere affection, the one does not experience sorrow, pain, or affliction of any kind, but the other's heart wishes to relieve, and vibrates in tenderness...like a well-organized musical instrument.*
> — Elizabeth Shaw

> *The Lord lives! Blessed be my Rock! Let the God of my salvation be exalted.*
> — Psalm 18:46

Having a sister is like having a best friend you can't get rid of. You know whatever you do, they'll still be there.

– Amy Li

> *You open your hand and satisfy the desire of every living thing.*
>
> – Psalm 145:16

JUST MY SISTERS AND *Me*
— AN INTRODUCTION

e were fortunate to grow up in
a family home with two parents
who loved and valued us. Our
childhood was fairly ordinary,
interlaced with the usual ups

and downs that life bestows. We were a household of women. Poor Dad . . . I guess that is why he always had "boy" dogs. That way, he was not quite so outnumbered.

Dianne is the youngest and probably the sanest of us all. Her common sense and insightful approach to life never ceases to amaze me. She has the uncanny ability to see the reality of a situation. More than once, she has brought me back to earth with her straightforward and sound advice.

Her days are filled with activities that often revolve around her husband and two growing boys. She often jokes about the hardship of being the only woman in the house, but through it all, her pride in her men is evident. Di is my rock. Whether times are good or bad, she is always there.

Patti is the middle child and I often think that

her personality reflects this. She is the flamboyant one . . . never afraid to take on a new challenge or adventure. This has not always led her down the safest of roads but with her, life is never dull.

Patti has a certain flare, and this is evident in both her dress and her life style. If anyone can frustrate me, it is Patti, but she has also taught me to respect another's viewpoint. She has a heart of gold and is not afraid to do things her way.

Distance separates all three of us. Many times I have wished that we lived closer, or at least in the same city. I would love to visit them on a whim . . . just for coffee and a chat. The times that we do spend together are precious and very much anticipated. Life is not always rosy between us, but even through the rough times, there is the knowledge that we are sisters and always there for each other.

MY *Sister*

y sister is my heart.
She opens doors to rooms
I never knew were there,
Breaks through walls
I don't recall building.
She lights my darkest corners
With the sparkle in her eyes.
My sister is my soul.

She inspires my wearied spirit
To fly on wings of angels
But while I hold her hand
My feet never leave the ground.
She stills my deepest fears
With the wisdom of her song.
My sister is my past.
She writes my history
In her eyes I recognize myself,
Memories only we can share.
She remembers, she forgives
She accepts me as I am
With tender understanding.
My sister is my future.
She lives within my dreams
She sees my undiscovered secrets,
Believes in me as I stumble

She walks in step beside me,
Her love lighting my way.
My sister is my strength
She hears the whispered prayers
That I cannot speak
She helps me find my smile,
Freely giving hers away
She catches my tears
In her gentle hands.
My sister is like no one else
She's my most treasured friend
Filling up the empty spaces
Healing broken places
She is my rock, my inspiration.
Though impossible to define,
In a word, she is . . . my sister. [17]

"Is solace anywhere more comforting than in the arms of a sister?

– Alice Walker

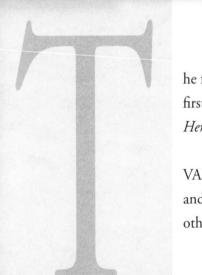

LONG-LOST SISTERS FIND EACH OTHER IN VALDOSTA *Reunited*

The following fascinating story was first printed in the *Athens Banner-Herald*, May 3, 2003:

VALDOSTA — Mamie Mann and Clara Mahan walked in each other's footsteps for nearly 73 years before the two lost sisters found each other, reunited after being separated since the Great Depression.

After years of searching, the Internet finally brought together Mann, 76, of Van Buren, Arkansas, with her sister, Mahan, 81, of Valdosta, Georgia.

Mann was only three and one-half years old when she was taken to an orphanage in Helena, Oklahoma, with her ten-year-old brother around 1930.

By the time Mahan, then eight years old, went to the orphanage just a few months later, Mann was gone. She had already been adopted by a German couple, who changed her birthdate and her name from Mary Elizabeth Dobson to Mamie Styckee.

Mahan said her parents sent the children to an orphanage because they could not provide for a family of four boys and two girls, and because their mother was sick.

Mann lived on a farm with her adoptive family in Pauls Valley, Oklahoma, until she was 12 when they moved to Arkansas. Mahan was moved to a foster home in Buffalo, Oklahoma.

"I was so unhappy there, I cried the whole year," she said. "I went to the second foster home in Lahoma, Oklahoma, and lived there until I married."

Ever since, they have followed one another without ever knowing it. The sisters came within a two-minute drive of each other when Mahan vacationed yearly in Oklahoma. They both crochet afghans and give them to their kids. They worked in nursing. They enjoy cooking.

It wasn't until 1971 that the two started looking for each other. Mann couldn't try sooner because her adoptive parents wouldn't talk about her biological family.

"Every effort I made was a dead end," she said. "Neither one of us knew how to go about it."

Mahan's daughter-in-law renewed the search in 1999 when she put a notice on the Internet saying Mahan was searching for a younger sister adopted out of an orphanage in Helena.

On Mann's end, a friend put her in touch with a researcher to help her find her lost family. When Mann asked the researcher, Linda Colvard, about Helena, she knew she was on the right track.

"Oh, my goodness. Oh, my goodness," Colvard said, telling Mann about the notice from Mahan searching from her sister.

The 1930 census, which was recently released on the Internet, confirmed Mann and Mahan were related.

Mann called Mahan and said, "I think this is your little sister, Mary."

Mahan replied, "I know it is."

The two met in Van Buren, and then again in Valdosta on Thursday.

"I waited almost 73 years to see my sister," Mann said.

"It was very emotional," Mahan said. "It's a miracle."[18]

Of two sisters one is always the watcher, one the dancer.
                                                    – Louise Gluck

Take firm hold of instruction, do not let go; keep her, for she is your life.

                                                    – Proverbs 4:13

FIRST PERSON: SISTERHOOD OF THE *Sisters*

To Sis

e're off!" I hollered to my younger sister as our airplane rose into the air, leaving our brothers and parents far behind. We smiled at each other, eagerly anticipating the six-week summer vacation to Spain and France with our aunt, uncle and cousins.

By the time we disembarked 15 hours later, we could barely contain our excitement. It was our first time in Europe, and everywhere we looked there were strange foods to sample, cute clothes to try on, museums to explore and wide-open countryside to bike through.

The first few days, however, were not easy. My sister, Janelle, and I began to miss our family and friends back home. We fought sometimes, squabbling over petty issues now long forgotten. But then things began to change. I distinctly remember one late night after a fight, when we both could not sleep, that began as an apology session but ended in the sharing of secrets, dreams and wishes. Janelle revealed her insecurities about beginning high school, and I told her my fear of having many good friends yet no true best friend who really knew me deeply. The next morning, few words were exchanged, yet we had clearly reached a new understanding.

The days whizzed by and even the hardships seemed less burdensome. When we misread the bike-route notes and found ourselves in the middle of a cornfield with a farmer who spoke only Catalan, we found the way back together. When Janelle became frustrated over navigating the Spanish language, I was by her side to assist her. When I slipped down the stone steps of an ancient castle, she was there to pick me up. We spent all of our free time together, playing in the waves of the nearby beaches, walking around the towns and shopping for souvenirs.

Then one day, Janelle became ill. I stayed near her until late at night, when I finally drifted off. I awoke shivering, my head pounding and my stomach aching.

We were both very ill for more than a week, and in the confines of our hotel room we had no one but each other to rely on. Together we slowly recovered, passing the time reading to each other, laughing at dumb Spanish cartoons, groaning at the bland soup we had to eat and reassuring each other that it would soon be over.

Perhaps it was the sickness more than anything else that cemented our relationship. Upon returning to the States, we discovered that we had become inseparable. Though we both hang out with many friends from school and soccer, the time we share as sisters is somehow different. We stay up late, chatting in our bunk beds. We go to the mall, play soccer and stress over homework together. It is reassuring to always have a friend at home. I can tell Janelle anything — from new Elvish words I've learned to my problems with friends at school to my doubts about college.

Yet there is one issue I have never again confided to her — the desire to find a best friend. For I now realize that a sister is the truest and most sincere friend anyone could ever have.[19]

> *How do people make it through life without a sister?*
>
> – Sara Corpening

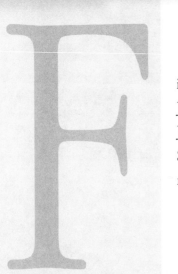

"The *Notestine* Girls"

All six of Them mark National Sister's Day

F ifty years ago, the call for "Jane, Joan, Janet, Joyce, Judy and Joy" could be heard throughout Sunbury's North River Avenue neighborhood.

The person behind the call was Mid Notestine. Jane, Joan, Janet, Joyce, Judy and Joy are known in the community as "the Notestine girls," but to each other they are much more — they are sisters.

National Sister's Day is today, but the Notestine girls have been celebrating their own version of Sister's Day for years.

"We didn't know there was an official day set aside for sisters," said Joan Notestine. "We just love being together."

One of her sisters, Janet Mull of Sunbury, explained that their mother raised her children — who, along with their brother John Campbell, all still live in Sunbury except Jane, who lives in Lewisburg — with much pride. "We were very poor," said Janet, "but we never knew it until we were older. Mom made it so we didn't miss out on anything. We were raised to believe that money wasn't everything."

The Notestine girls, who include twins Leah Jane Stein and Joan Notestine, attribute their upbringing for the closeness they have shared all these years. "Even though there were seven children, Mom made us each feel special," said Janet. "Mom touched so many lives and taught us, through her example, good values, honesty and compassion."

When asked to describe the bond, "love" was the unanimous word. Jane (who often goes by Leah Jane) took this a step further — "Some people change and forget to tell each other; we are always there, hidden behind our lives waiting to share, never alone."

"And don't forget our special whistle," said Joyce Osman.

Joyce explained that whenever their mother would drive by one of the girls' homes, she would do "the Notestine whistle" just to let them know she was thinking about them. "Now we all whistle," said Joyce. "We may not have time to stop and visit, but we always have time to whistle — just our little way of saying I love you, and keep Mom's memory alive."

Joyce added, "We love each other unconditionally — all seven J's." Janet said it wasn't until recently that their brother, Johnny, told them that he sometimes felt left out while growing up with six sisters.

"We had no idea he felt that way," said Janet.

John Campbell said growing up in a house filled with girls was never dull.

"I couldn't be happier to have these six women as my sisters," he said. "I never remember a time growing up when we weren't happy — our mother always saw to that."

The sisters remember their mom, who died in

1994, by continuing childhood traditions.

"Eating onion sandwiches and black licorice," said Joyce. "Sitting in a row and combing each other's hair while Mom read the Bible," added Joy Zeiders. And "singing and dancing," they all said at once.

"We now incorporate these childhood memories into the lives of our children, grandchildren and great-grandchildren," said Janet.

Together the six sisters have 16 children, 32 grandchildren and soon-to-be six great-grandchildren.[20]

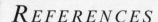

REFERENCES

1 Monica Rountree-Johnson

2 Lauren Lawson Leaston

3 W.H. Davies

4 Monica S.

5 Sister Stories website, by Ginger Andrews

6 Karl Augustus Menninger

7 Melissa Knapp, Heartwarmers4u

8 Lynn Lombard, Source Unknown

9 Terri Vandermark, *Chicken Soup for the Teenage Soul*

10 by: Timothy David, Source Unknown

11 Kelly, Heartwarmers4u

12 Eddie Ogan, collected on the Internet

13 "Sisters," Copyright 1953 by Irving Berlin.

14 June Deay Benton

[15] Brenda Looney

[16] *Woman's World*

[17] Poem by Lisa Lorden

[18] Associated Press, published in the *Athens Banner-Herald* on Saturday, May 3, 2003

[19] Jennifer Neczypor

[20] By Debra Brubaker, for *The Daily Item*

Photo Credits